MARTINI

- 2 1/2 ounces gin or vodka
- 1/2 ounce dry vermouth
- Lemon peel twist or olives, for garnish
- Ice

SINGAPORE SLING

- 1/2 oz grenadine syrup
- 1 oz gin
- sweet and sour mix
  maraschino cherry
- 2 ounces club soda
- 1 ounce Benedictine
- 1 ounce lime juice
- 1 1/2 ounces gin

MAI TAI

- 1 oz light rum
- 1/2 oz creme de almond
- 1/2 oz triple sec
- sweet and sour mix
- pineapple juice
- 1/2 oz Dark rum

SEA BREEZE

- 4 oz Cranberry juice
- 1 oz Grapefruit juice
- 1.75 oz Vodka

TOM COLLINS

- 2 oz gin
- 1 oz lemon juice
- 1 tsp superfine sugar
- 1 slice orange
- 3 oz club soda
- 1 maraschino cherry

OLD FASHIONED

- 2 oz rye or bourbon
- 2 dashes Angostura bitters
- 1 sugar cabe
- club soda

COTTON CANDY FRAPPE

- 2 Tablespoons of Vanilla Syrup
- 1/2 Cup of Vanilla Bean Ice Cream
- 3 Tablespoons of Raspberry Syrup
- Whipped Cream Topping
- 2/3 Cup of Milk
- 1 1/2 Cup of Ice

COOKIE FRAPPE

- 1/4 cup Milk
- 10-12 ice cubes
- 5-6 oreo biscuits
- 1 tablespoon chocolate chips
- 2 tablespoon chocolate sauce
- 1/4 teaspoon instant coffee powder
- 3 scoops vanilla ice cream
- Whipping cream topping

BIRTHDAY CAKE FRAPPE

- 2 Tablespoons Hazelnut Syrup
- 3-4 Tablespoons Vanilla Syrup
- 1 Tablespoon simple syrup
- Cake Sprinkles topping
- Pinch of Xantham Gum
- 3/4 Cup Milk
- 2 Cup Ice

CARAMEL FRAPPE

- 1 teaspoon Vanilla
- 1/2 Cup black coffee, cooled
- 2 Tablespoons Caramel sauce
- Whipped cream and caramel sauce topping
- 4 Cup Ice
- 1/4 Cup of Milk

S'MORES FRAPPE

- 1 tablespoon whipped cream topping
- 2 tablespoons marshmallow fluff
- 1/4 cup cold coffee
- 1 cup vanilla ice cream
- 1/2 cup milk
- 1 tablespoon chocolate syrup
- 2 tablespoons s'mores syrup
- 1 cup ice

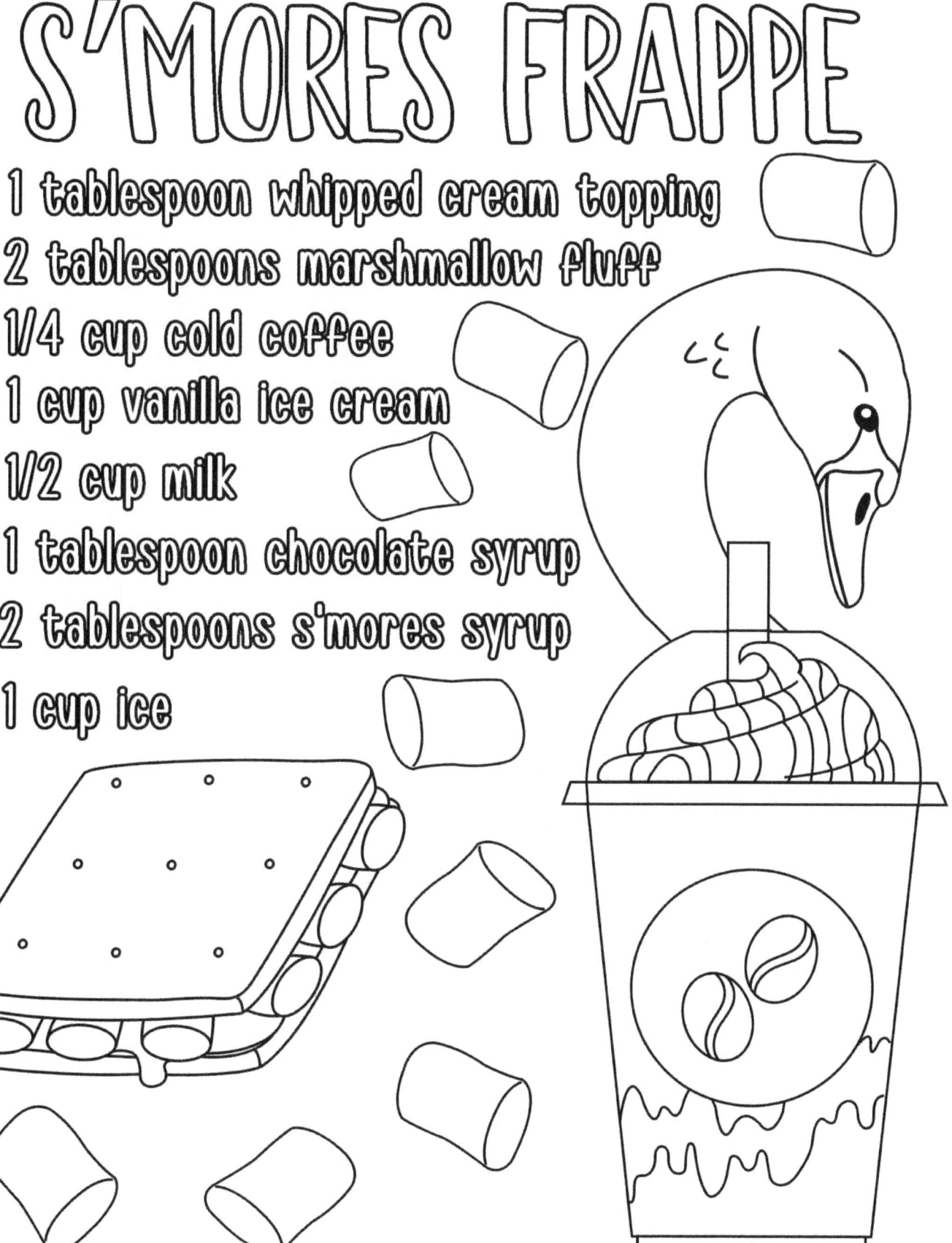

RED VELVET FRAPPE

- 2 oz espresso or strongly brewed coffee
- 2 scoops vanilla ice cream
- 1 oz red food coloring
- Whipped cream topping
- 1 tbsp cocoa
- 5 oz milk
- 1 cup ice

APPLE - GINGER SMOOTHIE

- Blend 1 chopped peeled apple
- a 1/2-inch piece peeled ginger
- the juice of 2 limes
- 1 cup water
- 2 cups ice
- 1/4 cup honey

BLUEBERRY - BANANA SMOOTHIE

- 1/2 cup unsweetened coconut milk
- 1/4 teaspoon almond extract
- 1 tablespoon each honey and lime juice
- 1 cup blueberries
- Blend 1 banana
- 1 cup ice

BLACK RASPBERRY-VANILLA SMOOTHIE

- Blend 1 pint blackberries
- 1/2 cup raspberries
- 1 cup vanilla yogurt
- 1 tablespoon honey

APPLE-SPINACH SMOOTHIE

- 1 chopped peeled apple, 1/2 cup silken tofu
- 1/4 cup each soy milk and orange juice
- 1 tablespoon each wheat germ
- honey and lemon juice
- 1 cup ice

LEMON-POPPY SEED SMOOTHIE

- Blend 2 teaspoons poppy seeds
- the zest and juice of 1/2 lemon
- 1 cup plain yogurt
- 1/3 cup sugar
- 1/2 cup each milk
- ice

PEANUT BUTTER- BANANA SMOOTHIE

- 1/2 teaspoon cocoa powder
- 2 tablespoons malted milk powder
- 1/2 cup creamy peanut butter
- 1 cup vanilla yogurt
- 1/3 cup milk
- a pinch of salt
- Blend 1 banana
- 2 cups ice

CUCUMBER- KALE SMOOTHIE

- Blend 1 1/4 cups vegetable juice
- 1/2 peeled cucumber
- 3 kale leaves
- the juice of 1/2 lemon

SPICED PUMPKIN SMOOTHIE

- Blend 1/2 cup each pumpkin puree
- 3 1/2 tablespoons brown sugar
- 1/2 teaspoon pumpkin pie spice
- a pinch of salt
- 1 cup milk
- 1 cup ice

APRICOT-ALMOND SMOOTHIE

- Blend 1 1/2 cups apricot nectar
- 1/2 cup vanilla yogurt
- 2 tablespoons almond butter
- 1 cup ice

KIWI-STRAWBERRY SMOOTHIE

- Blend 1 cup strawberries
- 2 tablespoons sugar
- 2 peeled kiwis
- 2 cups ice

Printed in the USA
CPSIA information can be obtained
at www.ICGtesting.com
CBHW080131021024
15218CB00028B/1235